I CAN COUNT

YOUNG & GIFTED SERIES

THIS BOOK BELONGS TO:

_____

ONE

TWO

2

THREE

3

FOUR

FIVE

5

SIX

6

SEVEN

7

EIGHT

8

NINE

TEN

10

ELEVEN

11

TWELVE

12

THIRTEEN

13

FOURTEEN

14

FIFTEEN

15

SIXTEEN

16

SEVENTEEN

17

EIGHTEEN

18

NINETEEN

19

TWENTY

20

Find the Young & Gifted Serie wherever books are sold